Instant RabbitMQ Messaging Application Development How-to

Build scalable message-based applications with RabbitMQ

Andrew Keig

[PACKT] PUBLISHING

BIRMINGHAM - MUMBAI

Instant RabbitMQ Messaging Application Development How-to

First published: May 2013

Production Reference: 1150513

Published by Packt Publishing Ltd.
Livery Place
35 Livery Street
Birmingham B3 2PB, UK.

ISBN 978-1-78216-574-3

www.packtpub.com

Credits

Author
Andrew Keig

Reviewer
Chris Duncan

Acquisition Editor
Andrew Duckworth

Commissioning Editor
Shreerang Deshpande

Technical Editor
Amit Ramadas

Project Coordinator
Suraj Bist

Proofreader
Clyde Jenkins

Graphics
Abhinash Sahu

Production Coordinator
Arvindkumar Gupta

Cover Work
Arvindkumar Gupta

Cover
Nitesh Thakur

About the Author

Andrew Keig has been building web applications for over 12 years. Andrew has a degree in Computing and blogs at `blog.airasoul.net` on topics he is passionate about, such as Node.js, REST, Web APIs, and Behavior-driven development. He also contributes to various Node.js open source projects. Andrew is a director at Airasoul, which specializes in the design and build of scalable, RESTful, specification-driven, and real-time web-based applications on the Node.js stack. His recent contracts include Starcount, ITV, Disney, Haymarket, and Live Nation to name a few.

Acknowledgement

This book is dedicated to my son and best friend Indie; I love you.

I would like to thank my wife Rima for her love and support during the writing of this book. I thank my parents and the rest of my family and friends for their support, with a special thank you to my brother, Graham, for inspiring me. Hopefully, authoring this book will inspire the next generation of my family; Indie, Bradley, Ellie, Som, Sachi, and Ruthi to achieve even greater things.

Finally, I would like to thank the AMQP and RabbitMQ teams, Ryan Dahl, Theo Schlossnagle, and all of the node-amqp committers; Suraj Bist, Shreerang Deshpande, and Amit Ramadas at Packt Publishing for their support. A big thank you to our technical reviewer Chris Duncan for his input; my work colleagues of the past and present; Johnny Hall and everyone at Starcount, Carl Hörberg at CloudAMQP, Gavin Van Der Merwe, and Joe Mendonca at Disney, and Rob Taylor at ITV.

About the Reviewer

Chris Duncan is an IT consultant with over 20 years of experience in the industry, who enjoys helping businesses to take advantage of software as a service and open source solutions. He has worked for various organizations, both large and small, including the European Commission in Brussels. Chris is the author of Bunny, a popular Ruby AMQP client, and has been using RabbitMQ ever since he discovered it while searching for a cost-effective alternative to other expensive messaging middleware products.

Table of Contents

Preface

Building software applications that are scalable, reliable, responsive, able to adapt to change, and solve the interoperability problem is non-trivial. Achieving such a system using open standards before the introduction of AMQP (Advanced Message Queuing Protocol) complicated things further. Now with an AMQP message broker such as RabbitMQ, we can all take the advantage of message-based systems, which up until recently were only accessible to large corporates.

What this book covers

What can RabbitMQ do for you? helps you to understand reasons for using a message broker, including a brief of history of AMQP (Advanced Message Queuing Protocol).

Installing RabbitMQ (Simple) gives you instructions on how to set up, manage, configure and monitor RabbitMQ.

Installing Node.js (Simple) gives you instructions on how to setup Node.js and NPM, and also guides you through the process of building a simple Node.js Hello World application.

Hello World (Simple) guides you through the process of building a simple RabbitMQ-based Hello World application. We also look at our options for monitoring AMQP, and set up the RabbitMQ management plugin.

Work Queues (Intermediate) introduces the remainder of this book, and begins to decouple a highly-coupled e-commerce shop using messaging patterns. We start with Work Queues, distributing time-consuming tasks among multiple workers.

Persistent messages (Intermediate) begins the first of the three tasks looking at reliable message delivery. This task guides you through the process of enabling durable messages on our e-commerce shop.

Acknowledgements (Intermediate) further examines reliable message delivery by enabling message acknowledgements.

Publisher Confirms (Intermediate) completes the previous section on reliable message delivery enabling a RabbitMQ extension to AMQP and a replacement for AMQPs transaction mechanism, which guarantees message delivery.

Publish Subscribe (Advanced) continues our journey and implements another messaging pattern, Publish Subscribe, which allows us to easily distribute a message to multiple consumer applications.

Complex routing (Advanced) completes our decoupling process and implements a variation of the Publish Subscribe pattern, allowing us to route different types of messages to multiple queues.

Go forth and multiply completes our journey by discussing a series of further topics to research and consider when building and deploying applications using RabbitMQ.

What you need for this book

In order to create and run the examples in this book, you will need a MAC or a PC running either Windows or Linux; you can use any text editor. This book will provide you with instructions on installing RabbitMQ, Node.js, NPM, and Wireshark, and the RabbitMQ client for Node.js, node-amqp.

Who this book is for

This book targets developers who want to build scalable message-based applications using RabbitMQ in any language. The examples in this book are written in Node.js, a server-side JavaScript platform for building fast scalable network applications. No knowledge of RabbitMQ or Node.js is required; The reader is expected to have a rudimentary understanding of JavaScript or other high-level languages.

Conventions

In this book, you will find a number of styles of text that distinguish between different kinds of information. Here are some examples of these styles, and an explanation of their meaning.

Code words in text are shown as follows: "The `require('util')` statement returns us access to the methods exported from the Node.js core module `util`."

A block of code is set as follows:

```
var util = require('util');

exports.hello = function hello() {
    util.puts('Hello world');
}
```

When we wish to draw your attention to a particular part of a code block, the relevant lines or items are set in bold:

```
this.Checkout = function() {
    console.log("INFO, Placed order " +
  this.Order.OrderId);
  this.ProcessOrder(); //remove
 };
 this.ProcessOrder = function() {
     this.PaymentGateway();
     this.UpdateStatus();
     if (this.Status === 'OrderComplete') {
         this.UpdateInventory();
         this.SendEmail();
         this.UpdateReporting();
     }
     console.log('INFO, Thank you for placing your order...');
 };
```

Any command-line input or output is written as follows:

```
rabbitmq-server
```

New terms and **important words** are shown in bold. Words that you see on the screen, in menus or dialog boxes for example, appear in the text like this: "There are tabbed options for viewing **Connections**, **Channels**, **Exchanges**, and **Queues**."

> Warnings or important notes appear in a box like this.

> Tips and tricks appear like this.

Reader feedback

Feedback from our readers is always welcome. Let us know what you think about this book—what you liked or may have disliked. Reader feedback is important for us to develop titles that you really get the most out of.

To send us general feedback, simply send an e-mail to `feedback@packtpub.com`, and mention the book title via the subject of your message.

If there is a topic that you have expertise in and you are interested in either writing or contributing to a book, see our author guide on www.packtpub.com/authors.

Customer support

Now that you are the proud owner of a Packt book, we have a number of things to help you to get the most from your purchase.

Downloading the example code

You can download the example code files for all Packt books you have purchased from your account at http://www.packtpub.com. If you purchased this book elsewhere, you can visit http://www.packtpub.com/support and register to have the files e-mailed directly to you.

Errata

Although we have taken every care to ensure the accuracy of our content, mistakes do happen. If you find a mistake in one of our books—maybe a mistake in the text or the code—we would be grateful if you would report this to us. By doing so, you can save other readers from frustration and help us improve subsequent versions of this book. If you find any errata, please report them by visiting http://www.packtpub.com/submit-errata, selecting your book, clicking on the **errata submission form** link, and entering the details of your errata. Once your errata are verified, your submission will be accepted and the errata will be uploaded on our website, or added to any list of existing errata, under the Errata section of that title. Any existing errata can be viewed by selecting your title from http://www.packtpub.com/support.

Piracy

Piracy of copyright material on the Internet is an ongoing problem across all media. At Packt, we take the protection of our copyright and licenses very seriously. If you come across any illegal copies of our works, in any form, on the Internet, please provide us with the location address or website name immediately so that we can pursue a remedy.

Please contact us at copyright@packtpub.com with a link to the suspected pirated material.

We appreciate your help in protecting our authors, and our ability to bring you valuable content.

Questions

You can contact us at questions@packtpub.com if you are having a problem with any aspect of the book, and we will do our best to address it.

Instant RabbitMQ Messaging Application Development How-to

Welcome to *Instant RabbitMQ Messaging Application Development How-to*. This book will give you a quick, step-by-step introduction to the world of RabbitMQ and will demonstrate reasons for using RabbitMQ as I guide you through the process of decoupling a highly coupled e-commerce application using various messaging patterns, allowing us to scale, improving responsiveness, performance, throughput, and efficiency.

This book targets developers looking to take advantage of RabbitMQ as a message broker on any platform using any language. The examples in this book are written in server-side JavaScript with Node.js.

Head over to GitHub and clone/download the example source code repository for this book from `www.github.com/AndrewKeig/rabbitmq-messaging-application-development`.

What can RabbitMQ do for you?

RabbitMQ (`www.rabbitmq.com`) is an open source message broker that implements version 0-9-1 of the **AMQP** (**Advanced Message Queuing Protocol**). It is an open standard, networking wire-level protocol, which allows client applications that conform to the AMQP standard, to communicate with AMQP brokers. For more information on the AMQP standard, read the specifications at `https://www.rabbitmq.com/resources/specs/amqp0-9-1.pdf`.

AMQP originated in the financial services industry. Its main aim was to define an interoperable messaging protocol which allowed organizations to move away from expensive vendor-specific messaging implementations without breaking existing applications.

The RabbitMQ implementation of AMQP was developed and supported through Rabbit Technologies Ltd., a joint venture between Lshift and Cohesive Flexible Technologies. RabbitMQ is now maintained by SpringSource, a division of VMware. The RabbitMQ server is written in Erlang and is built on the Open Telecom Platform framework: `erlang-solutions.com`.

Message brokers enable software applications to connect to each other as components of a larger application. The reasons for using a message broker are as follows:

- **Scalability**: Distribute time-consuming tasks among multiple workers
- **Responsiveness**: Process tasks asynchronously and improve response times
- **Availability**: Cluster applications for improved availability of service
- **Complexity**: Decoupling simplifies application development
- **Efficiency**: Avoid polling for changes with publish/subscribe
- **Extendability**: Add new services which respond to existing messages
- **Interoperability**: Write systems composed of services written in different languages
- **Maintainability**: Maintain/take down your application without losing messages
- **Robustness**: Defer data consumption without fear of losing data
- **Reliability**: Persist and acknowledge messages for improved reliability

Installing RabbitMQ (Simple)

Messaging with RabbitMQ is simple. There, I said it. Once you have completed reading this book, you will with confidence be able to state the same.

Getting ready

RabbitMQ supports a vast number of operating systems. In this task, we will install and start-up a RabbitMQ server. We will also describe the AMQP model, the protocol that RabbitMQ implements.

How to do it...

The RabbitMQ installation steps vary based on your operating systems and preferred method of installation. We will not repeat the installation steps here, as there are detailed instructions on the RabbitMQ website for all platforms. If you are on a Linux variant, it's possible you already have RabbitMQ installed.

RabbitMQ has a dependency on Erlang, the language used to write RabbitMQ. You may need to install Erlang first if its not already installed on your machine. So, get yourselves over to the RabbitMQ download page (`www.rabbitmq.com/download.html`) and install RabbitMQ for your environment.

> If, after installation, you have not added RabbitMQ to your environment path, please navigate to your RabbitMQ installation folder before running commands against the RabbitMQ server. The RabbitMQ server and command-line tools are located in the `sbin` subfolder.

1. In order to start the RabbitMQ server open a command-line shell, and type the following command. You may need to run this command with elevated privileges.

   ```
   rabbitmq-server
   ```

   The following is a screenshot of the RabbitMQ start-up screen. It includes useful information such as the node name and path to RabbitMQ's log files, which are useful for debugging your messaging applications:

2. Running `rabbitmq-server` with the `-detached` flag will run rabbit as a background process.

   ```
   rabbitmq-server -detached
   ```

3. In order to stop the RabbitMQ server, type the following command:

```
rabbitmqctl stop
```

> An alternative way of stopping a process from a command shell is to use the key combination *Ctrl* + *C* (`SIGINT`). The *Ctrl* + *Z* (`SIGTSTP`) key combination on POSIX-based systems (Mac OS X/Linux) should not be used. This key combination will suspend the process, not stop the process. This will become important when we work with multiple consumers.

4. To view the status of the RabbitMQ server type the following command:

```
rabbitmqctl status
```

> If the RabbitMQ server is not running, all `rabbitmqctl` commands will report the node as nodedown as follows:
>
> **Error: unable to connect to node rabbit@localhost: nodedown**

The task `Hello World` includes more information on managing a RabbitMQ server, both from the command line and via the management UI.

How it works...

AMQP 0-9-1 is a programmable message protocol that allows **producers** to distribute messages to **consumers**. The model works like so: messages are published by producers to **exchanges**, and exchanges distribute messages to **queues** using rules called **bindings**.

An AMQP broker will deliver messages to consumers subscribed to queues, or consumers fetch/pull messages from queues on demand. **Virtual hosts** (**vhosts**) make it possible for a single broker to host multiple isolated mini RabbitMQ environments. The following diagram explains the concept:

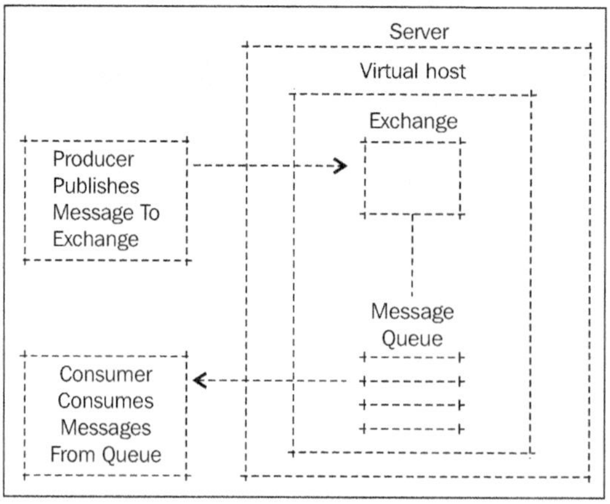

An AMQP broker declares a single instance of each exchange type for every virtual host. These exchanges are named with a concatenation of a prefix of `amq.` with the exchange type, for example: `amq.topic`. The table below lists the exchanges:

name	durable	type	auto_delete
	True	direct	False
amq.direct	True	direct	False
amq.fanout	True	fanout	False
amq.headers	True	headers	False
amq.match	True	headers	False
amq.topic	True	topic	False

The empty default exchange (AMQP default) is an `amq.direct` exchange. The broker will declare a binding between the default exchange and every queue in the system, with the binding key being identical to the queue name. So when we publish a message to the default exchange, we simply specify a routing key being equal to the queue name.

Installing Node.js (Simple)

In order to build messaging applications with RabbitMQ, we need to select a programming language and a RabbitMQ client. There are many RabbitMQ clients in many languages, including Ruby, Python, Java, and .NET. This book will use **Node.js** and the world's most popular programming language, **JavaScript**.

Getting ready

Node.js is a server-side platform for building fast, scalable network applications. Built on Google Chrome's V8 JavaScript engine, Node.js is a single-threaded process that uses an event-driven, non-blocking I/O model, making it ideal for real-time applications. Visit `www.nodejs.org` to learn more about Node.js.

How to do it...

There are installers on the Node.js website for Mac OS X and Windows users; Linux/Unix users should compile and run the source code. In order to set up Node.js, head over to `www.nodejs.org/download`; download and run the installer. For Linux/Unix users or the daring amongst you looking for instructions on compiling from source, visit the installation guide on the Node.js GitHub repository wiki, `www.github.com/joyent/node/wiki/Installation`.

Head over to GitHub and clone/download the example source code repository for this book from `www.github.com/AndrewKeig/rabbitmq-messaging-application-development`.

How it works...

Node.js programs are written in JavaScript. Node provides a small set of built-in core modules, which allow us to do things such as file I/O, TCP/IP, and create HTTP servers. A complete list of core modules are described in detail on the Node.js API page, `www.nodejs.org/api`.

Node.js has a simple module loading system to simplify the development of complex applications. Here is an example of a simple module that prints a message to the console. Let's navigate to our source code examples' folder and locate the folder `Installing-Node-js`; here you will find two files required for this task: `greetings.js` and `server.js`.

Let's look at the `greetings.js` file.

1. The `require('util')` statement returns us access to the methods exported from the Node.js core module `util`; the module is assigned to a variable `util`.
2. Our module contains a single function `hello`, which prints `Hello world` to the console:

```
var util = require('util');

exports.hello = function hello() {
    util.puts('Hello world');
}
```

> **Downloading the example code**
>
> You can download the example code files for all Packt books you have purchased from your account at `http://www.packtpub.com`. If you purchased this book elsewhere, you can visit `http://www.packtpub.com/support` and register to have the files e-mailed directly to you.

3. The functions and variables within a Node.js module are private. You can expose its functions and variables by populating the `exports` object, which we do here by assigning our function to a property on the `exports` object `hello`.

Let's look at the `server.js` file.

1. We include the `greetings.js` module and assign it to a variable. Notice that the path includes `./`; this signifies a relative file path and a local module.
2. We then execute the `hello` function:

```
var greetings = require('./greetings');
greetings.hello();
```

3. Open a command-line shell and run the application using the following command:

```
node server.js
```

Our node application prints `Hello world` to the console window—in the Node.js style.

There's more...

The Node.js installation includes a package manager called **Node Package Manager** (**NPM**). NPM is a command-line tool used to install new modules and manage a module's dependencies. Visit `www.npmjs.org` for more information on NPM.

Node.js programs include a `package.json` file, which exists in the root of a module. It tells NPM what dependencies the module requires in order to function. NPM will, when asked, install all dependencies listed in the dependencies section of the `package.json` file.

The following code snippet is the `package.json` file for the code examples in this book. You can see we have a dependency on a module - `amqp`, a RabbitMQ client for Node.js:

```
{
    "name": "packt-instant-rabbitmq"
  , "version": "0.0.1"
  , "dependencies": {
     "amqp": ">= 0.1.5"
  }
}
```

Let's go ahead and install the dependencies for our example source, which includes the RabbitMQ client `amqp`. The full title of the module is `node-amqp`; it's very simple to use and understand, and implements the majority of the 0-9-1 version of the AMQP protocol. Visit the NPM website `www.npmjs.org/package/amqp` for more information on this module.

Open your command-line shell, navigate to your source code example folder, and execute the following command:

```
npm install
```

This will install the dependencies listed in the `package.json` file.

Hello World (Simple)

Let's build a simple RabbitMQ-based `Hello World` application.

Getting ready

Navigate to your source code examples folder and locate the folder `Hello-World`. Here you will find two files: `producer.js` and `consumer.js` required for this task. Our `Hello World` application is simple; we have a producer which creates messages and sends them to an exchange, and the exchange delivers the messages to a queue. A consumer will read and process the messages from the queue.

How to do it...

Let's take a look at the `producer.js` script.

1. First, we import the `amqp` module and call `createConnection` on that module, returning a connection to the RabbitMQ server. This connection will have the following default properties:

   ```
   {host: 'localhost', port: 5672, login: 'guest', password: 'guest',
   vhost: '/'}
   ```

   For more information, navigate to `www.rabbitmq.com/uri-spec.html`.

2. Then, we create an array of `messages`.
3. We wait on a connection `ready` event.
4. When the connection `ready` event fires, we create an exchange. Here we use the default exchange, which is a direct exchange type.
5. We then create a queue named `'hello'`, and wait for a `queueDeclareOk` event to fire.
6. When the `queueDeclareOk` event fires, we bind the queue to the exchange using a binding key hash (`#`), which means to accept all messages delivered on the queue, ignoring the routing key. We then wait on the `queueBindOk` event.
7. When the event `queueBindOk` has fired, we publish our messages.
8. We loop through the messages; the `ex.publish` call publishes the message to the default exchange with a routing key `hello`.

   ```
   var connect = require('amqp').createConnection();
   var messages = [];
   messages.push(' (\\-/)');
   messages.push(" ('.')  -> hello world");
   ```

```
messages.push('(") (")');

connect.on('ready', function() {
    var ex = connect.exchange();
    var q = connect.queue('hello');
    q.on('queueDeclareOk', function(args) {
        q.bind('#');
        q.on('queueBindOk', function() {
            messages.forEach(function(message) {
                ex.publish('hello', message, {});
            });
        });
    });
});
```

Let us now take a look at the `consumer.js` script.

1. First, we import the `amqp` module and call `createConnection` on that module, returning a connection to the RabbitMQ server.
2. We wait on a connection `ready` event.
3. When the `ready` event fires, we create a queue called `'hello'` and wait for a `queueDeclareOk` event to be fired.
4. When the `queueDeclareOk` event is fired, we bind the queue to the exchange using a binding key hash (#), and we wait on the `queueBindOk` event.
5. When the event `queueBindOk` has fired, we subscribe to the queue, parse, and then print the incoming messages to the console.

```
var connect = require('amqp').createConnection();
connect.on('ready', function() {
  var q = connect.queue('hello');
  q.on('queueDeclareOk', function(args) {
      q.bind('#');
      q.on('queueBindOk', function() {
          q.subscribe(function(message) {
           console.log(message.data.toString());
          });
      });
  });
});
```

6. Open a command-line console and start RabbitMQ:

   `rabbitmq-server`

7. Open a command-line console, navigate to our source code examples folder, and locate the folder `Hello-World`. Execute the following command:

   `Hello-World> node consumer`

8. Open another command-line console, and again execute the following command:

   ```
   Hello-World> node producer
   ```

The following screenshot shows the output of running the `Hello World` consumer/producer application—in the RabbitMQ style.

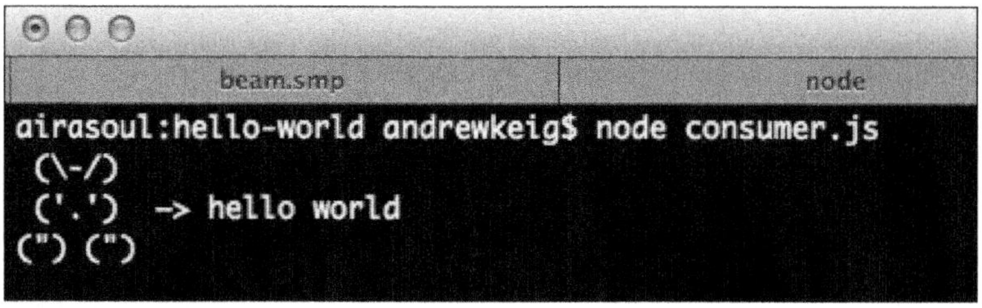

How it works...

AMQP 0-9-1 is structured as a logical grouping of AMQP methods. The AMQP 0-9-1 reference `www.rabbitmq.com/amqp-0-9-1-quickref.html` has a complete list of all the AMQP methods. If you would like to get under the covers and see the AMQP methods firing in real-time, consider using **Wireshark**, a network protocol analyzer that lets you capture and interactively browse the traffic running on a computer network. Wireshark allows you to monitor AMQP traffic by simply adding `amqp` to the filter. You can download Wireshark from `www.wireshark.org/download.html`.

Following is an example analysis of the consumer application from this task.

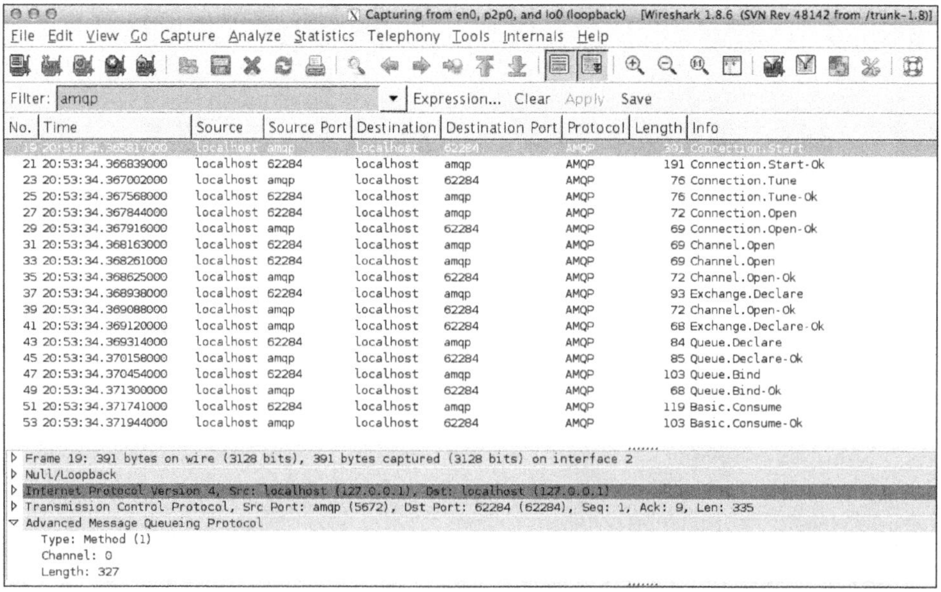

You can see in the **Info** column the various AMQP methods required in order to consume a message. Wireshark is a great tool for debugging AMQP-based messaging applications.

> The web-based UI port for RabbitMQ versions prior to 3.0 is 55672.

There's more...

The RabbitMQ management plugin (`www.rabbitmq.com/management.html`) enables management and monitoring of your RabbitMQ server. In order to install the RabbitMQ management plugin, run the following command from your RabbitMQ installation `sbin` subfolder:

```
rabbitmq-plugins enable rabbitmq_management
```

The management plugin includes three different methods for managing RabbitMQ:

- The web-based UI is located at `localhost:15672`
- The HTTP API and its documentation are both located `localhost:55672/api/`
- A command-line tool, rabbitmqadmin, located at `localhost:55672/cli/`

For more information navigate to `www.rabbitmq.com/management-cli.html`.

Let's login to the web-based UI:

Navigate to `http://server-name:15672` and enter the default username and password:

```
username guest
password: guest
```

When logged in you should see the following real-time overview of the RabbitMQ server. The overview includes the number of queued messages. There are tabbed options for viewing **Connections**, **Channels**, **Exchanges**, and **Queues**.

The CLI command-line tool can perform all of the functionalities available to you in the web-based management tool as follows:

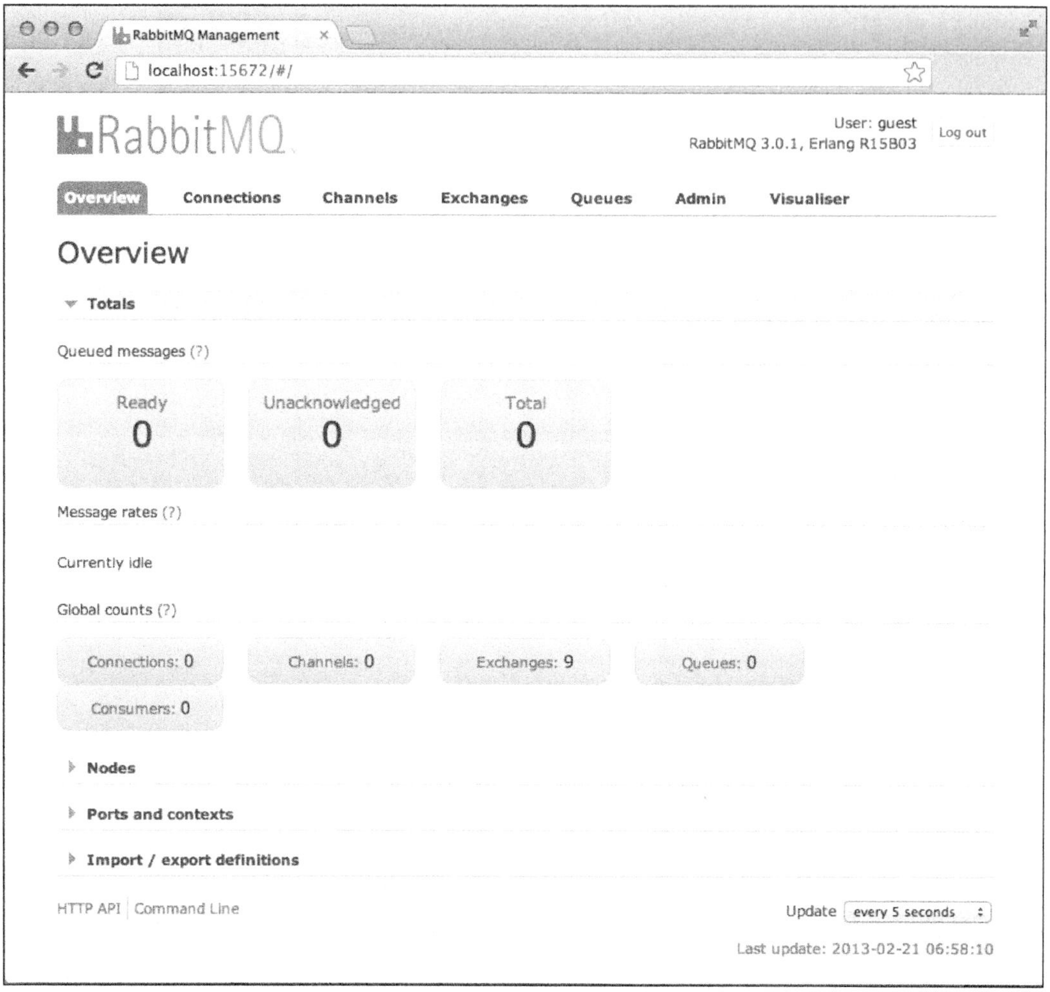

Let's again run the example from this chapter. Execute the following command to produce messages:

```
Hello-World> node producer
```

You should now see the number of queued messages on your management UI increase. If you run the following command, it will consume those messages and the number of queued messages will display **0**, emptying the queue.

```
Hello-World> node consumer
```

Please play around with the example and get comfortable with it. Add more messages to our `producer.js` script's `message` array.

Also try the command-line tool, rabbitmqadmin, which allows you to perform all of the same functions available to you via the management UI:

List all connections	`rabbitmqctl list_connections`
List all exchanges	`rabbitmqctl list_exchanges`
List all bindings	`rabbitmqctl list_bindings`
List all queues	`rabbitmqctl list_queues`
List all channels	`rabbitmqctl list_channels`

For a full list of commands, visit `www.rabbitmq.com/man/rabbitmqctl.1.man.html`.

AMQP is a multi-channeled protocol. The Node.js client node-amqp (unlike some other clients) abstracts away the concept of channels. Channels provide a way to multiplex a heavyweight TCP/IP connection into several lightweight connections. Whenever you create a queue or exchange with the node-amqp, you are creating a channel; exchanges and queues are a subclass of channel.

Work Queues (Intermediate)

Let's introduce the topic of the remainder of this book. sHop is a simplified but highly coupled e-commerce application. It contains a long running process that performs the following functions:

- `PaymentGateway`: Calls a payment gateway with credit card details
- `UpdateStatus`: Updates the order status; with success/failure
- `UpdateInventory`: Updates the catalog stock inventory
- `SendEmail`: Sends a confirmation email to the customer
- `UpdateReporting`: Updates the reporting analytics database

Getting ready

Let's navigate to our source code examples folder and locate the folder `Shop`. Here you will find our e-commerce application; it consists of three files, namely `order.js`, `orderService.js`, and `server.js`.

Let's take a look at the `order.js` script. This is a simple object with two properties, `OrderId` and `Status`.

```
module.exports = function order(orderId) {
    this.OrderId = orderId;
    this.Status = "Processing";
};
```

Let's take a look at the `orderService.js` script, which contains the order processor; the following has been simplified, so check the source code for a complete listing:

```
module.exports = function OrderService(order) {
    this.Order = order;
    this.Checkout = function() {
console.log("INFO, Placed order " +   this.Order.OrderId);
      this.ProcessOrder();
    };
    this.ProcessOrder = function() {
      this.PaymentGateway();
      this.UpdateStatus();
      if (this.Status === 'OrderComplete') {
          this.UpdateInventory();
          this.SendEmail();
          this.UpdateReporting();
       }
       console.log('INFO, Thank you for placing your order...');
    };
    this.PaymentGateway = function() {// see source };
    this.UpdateStatus = function() {// see source };
    this.UpdateInventory = function() {// see source };
    this.SendEmail = function() {// see source };
    this.UpdateReporting = function() {// see source };
};
```

Each of the preceding functions simply simulates doing actual work by printing a message.

The `server.js` script is our entry point and runs the `order` processor for a single order.

```
var order = require('./order');
var orderService = require('./orderService');
var service = new orderService(new order(1));
service.Checkout();
```

To run this program open a command-line console, navigate to our source code examples folder, and locate the folder `Shop`. Execute the following command:

```
sHop> node server
```

The following screenshot shows the output of running our sHop application.

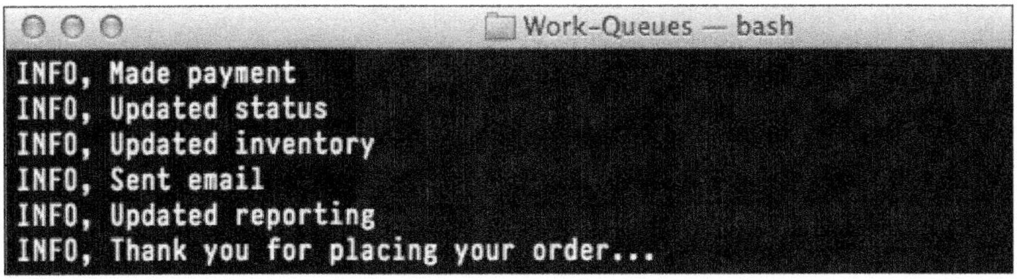

How to do it...

So how can we improve our application using messaging? The Work Queues pattern allows us to efficiently distribute time-consuming tasks among multiple workers. RabbitMQ will use a round-robin dispatch, sending each message to the next consumer in sequence.

What we need to do is split the application into two separate services: a service which simply starts the process by creating an order (producer), and a service that processes the order (consumer). Our producer application would simply add a message to a RabbitMQ queue. The message contains the order details, and then displays an `order` confirmation message. Our consumer service picks these messages off the queue and processes the order.

Let's review our existing sHop application and see what changes we need to make in order to implement Work Queues.

Take a look at the `orderService.js` script. In order to split this apart we remove the call to `ProcessOrder` from our `Checkout` method. Our producer application will call the `Checkout` function, and our consumer application will call the `ProcessOrder` function.

```
this.Checkout = function() {
     console.log("INFO, Placed order " +
   this.Order.OrderId);
   this.ProcessOrder(); //remove
 };
 this.ProcessOrder = function() {
     this.PaymentGateway();
     this.UpdateStatus();
     if (this.Status === 'OrderComplete') {
         this.UpdateInventory();
         this.SendEmail();
         this.UpdateReporting();
     }
     console.log('INFO, Thank you for placing your order...');
 };
```

Let's navigate to our source code examples folder and locate the folder `Work-Queues`. Take a look at the `producer.js` script.

1. First, we import the `order` and `orderService` modules.
2. Now, we import the `amqp` module and call `createConnection` on that module, returning a connection to the RabbitMQ server.
3. We also create an `orderId` variable and set it to `0`.
4. We wait on a connection `ready` event.
5. When the `ready` event fires, we create an exchange. We name the exchange `shop.exchange` and specify the exchange type `direct`.
6. We then create a queue and wait for a `queueDeclareOk` event to fire.
7. When the `queueDeclareOk` event is fired, we bind the queue to the exchange using a binding key `order.key`, and we wait on the `queueBindOk` event.
8. When the event `queueBindOk` is fired, we publish our messages.
9. We create an `order` and an `orderService`; we call `Checkout` on our service module, starting the `order` process.
10. The `exchange.publish` call publishes a message, which contains an order to the exchange with a routing key `order.key`. We repeat this indefinitely using `setInterval` for the purpose of this example to simulate lots of orders being placed:

```
var order = require('../shop/order');
var orderService = require('./orderService');
var connect = require('amqp').createConnection();
var orderId = 0;

connect.on('ready', function() {
   var ex = connect.exchange('shop.exchange',{type:'direct'});
    var q = connect.queue('shop.queue');
    q.on('queueDeclareOk', function(args) {
        q.bind('shop.exchange', 'order.key');
        q.on('queueBindOk', function() {
            console.log("Place your order");
            setInterval(function(){
              var newOrder = new order(++orderId);
              var service = new orderService(newOrder);
                service.Checkout();
                ex.publish('order.key',newOrder);}, 100);
        });
     });
   });
```

Take a look at the `consumer.js` script.

1. First, we import the `orderService` module.
2. Now, we import the `amqp` module and call `createConnection` on that module, returning a connection to the RabbitMQ server.
3. We wait on a connection `ready` event.
4. When the `ready` event fires, we create an exchange. We name the exchange `shop.exchange` and specify the exchange type `direct`.
5. We then create a queue and wait for a `queueDeclareOk` event to be fired.
6. When the `queueDeclareOk` event is fired, we bind the queue to the exchange using a binding key `order.key`, and we wait on the `queueBindOk` event.
7. When the event `queueBindOk` has fired, we read our messages from the queue.
8. We call the `subscribe` function on the queue and create an `orderService`, passing in the message details (our order). We then call the `ProcessOrder` function on our service module completing the order.

   ```
   var orderService = require('./orderService');
   var connect = require('amqp').createConnection();
   connect.on('ready', function() {
   var ex = connect.exchange('shop.exchange',{type:'direct'});
       var q = connect.queue('shop.queue');
       q.on('queueDeclareOk', function(args) {
           q.bind('shop.exchange', 'order.key');
           q.on('queueBindOk', function() {
               q.subscribe(function(message) {
                   var service = new orderService(message.data);
                   service.ProcessOrder();
               });
           });
       });
   });
   ```

9. If it's not running, open a command-line console and start RabbitMQ:

   rabbitmq-server

10. Open a command-line console, navigate to our source code examples folder, and locate the folder `Work-Queues`. Execute the following command:

    Work-Queues> node consumer

11. Open another command-line console, and execute the following command:

    ```
    Work-Queues> node producer
    ```

    RabbitMQ, like its namesake, is fast, but we can consume messages at an even faster rate.

12. Open another command-line console, navigate to our source code examples folder, and locate the folder `Work-Queues`. Execute the following command:

    ```
    Work-Queues> node consumer
    ```

We now have multiple consumers processing messages/orders; these consumers could exist on separate servers. We can horizontally scale, adding more consumers/servers with ease of improving the performance.

How it works...

Up until now we have used a Direct Exchange type; a Direct Exchange is also the default exchange. A Direct Exchange does an exact match between the routing key provided when publishing messages and the routing criteria used when a queue is bound to this exchange. The following diagram demonstrates the concept:

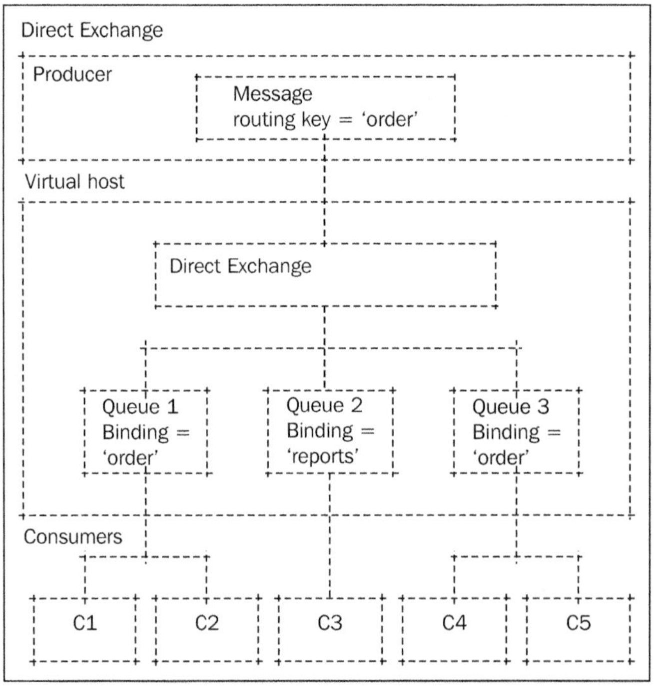

As you can see, a Direct Exchange can route messages to multiple queues with the same binding. From the preceding diagram we can see that the messages are routed to queues `1` and `3`.

Persistent messages (Intermediate)

Our sHop application is business critical. Losing sHop orders is not an option; we need to ensure every message is delivered and processed correctly. The next three tasks explore our options for reliable message delivery. This task will examine persistent messages.

Getting ready

If RabbitMQ stops for any reason, we will lose all of our exchanges, queues, and more importantly our messages (orders in our application).

In order to make sure that messages are not lost in the event of RabbitMQ restarting, we need to mark the queues durable and messages as persistent.

> If you make changes to the properties of exchanges and queues that already exist in the RabbitMQ server, our RabbitMQ client will throw an error when trying to connect. When starting this task and each new task, please remove all the data (messages, exchanges, and queues) from the RabbitMQ database, by executing the following commands:
>
> **rabbitmqctl stop_app**
> **rabbitmqctl reset**
> **rabbitmqctl start_app**

How to do it...

Let's navigate to our source code examples folder and locate the folder `Persistent-Messages`. These scripts simply builds on the code from the previous task. Take a look at the `producer.js` script and examine the changes made to persist messages.

1. The first change we have made is to set `durable` to `true` when creating a queue:

   ```
   var q = connect.queue('shop.queue', {durable:true});
   ```

2. We also mark our messages as persistent by supplying a `delivery_mode` property with a value `2`.

   ```
   ex.publish('order.key', newOrder, {deliveryMode:2});
   ```

Take a look at our `consumer.js` script:

1. When we create our queue, we set `durable` to `true`:

   ```
   var q = connect.queue('shop.queue', {durable:true});
   ```

Let's demonstrate this with the following set of commands:

1. Open a command-line console and start RabbitMQ:

   ```
   rabbitmq-server
   ```

2. Now open a command-line console, navigate to our source code examples folder, and locate the folder `Persistent-Messages`. Execute the following command:

   ```
   Persistent-Messages> node producer
   ```

Let the producer create several message/orders, press *Ctrl* + *C* while on the console to stop the producer creating orders.

1. Let's open another command-line console and run the `list_queues` command:

   ```
   rabbitmqctl list_queues
   ```

   The response should display shop queue; details include the name and the number of messages ready to be processed.

   ```
   Listing queues ...
   shop.queue 10
   ...done.
   ```

2. Now run the following command to stop and then restart RabbitMQ:

   ```
   rabbitmqctl stop
   rabbitmq-server
   ```

3. Now, again run the `list_queues` command. You will notice that the response still contains queues/messages:

   ```
   rabbitmqctl list_queues
   Listing queues ...
   shop.queue 10
   ...done.
   ```

> Marking messages as persistent tells RabbitMQ to persist the message to the disk. This does *not completely guarantee* that a message won't be lost. There exists a short time window when RabbitMQ has accepted a message and hasn't saved it, in which a RabbitMQ failure will result in a message being lost. Task Publisher Confirms will explore a solution to this.

Acknowledgements (Intermediate)

This task will examine reliable message delivery from the RabbitMQ server to a consumer.

Getting ready

If a consumer takes a message/order from our queue and the consumer dies, our unprocessed message/order will die with it.

In order to make sure a message is never lost, RabbitMQ supports **message acknowledgments** or **acks**. When a consumer has received and processed a message, an acknowledgment is sent to RabbitMQ from the consumer informing RabbitMQ that it is free to delete the message. If a consumer dies without sending an acknowledgment, RabbitMQ will redeliver it to another consumer.

How to do it...

Let's navigate to our source code examples folder and locate the folder `Message-Acknowledgement`. Take a look at the consumer.js script and examine the changes we have made to support acks.

1. We pass to the `{ack:true}` option to the `q.subscribe` function, which tells the queue that messages should be acknowledged before being removed:

   ```
   q.subscribe({ack:true}, function(message) {
   ```

2. When our message has been processed we call `q.shift`, which informs RabbitMQ that the message has been processed, and it can now be removed from the queue:

   ```
   q.shift();
   ```

> You can also use the `prefetchCount` option to increase the window of how many messages the server will send you before you need to send an acknowledgement. `{ack:true, prefetchCount:1}` is the default and will only send you one message before you acknowledge. Setting `prefetchCount` to `0` will make that window unlimited. A low value will impact performance, so it may be worth considering a higher value.

Let's demonstrate this concept.

1. Edit the consumer.js script located in the folder `Message-Acknowledgement`. Simply comment out the line `q.shift()`, which will stop the consumer from acknowledging the messages.
2. Open a command-line console and start RabbitMQ:

   ```
   rabbitmq-server
   ```

3. Now open a command-line console, navigate to our source code examples folder, and locate the folder `Message-Acknowledgement`. Execute the following command:

   ```
   Message-Acknowledgement> node producer
   ```

   Let the producer create several message/orders; press *Ctrl* + *C* while on the command-line console to stop the producer creating orders. Now execute the following to begin consuming messages:

   ```
   Message-Acknowledgement> node consumer
   ```

4. Let's open another command-line console and run `list_queues`:

   ```
   rabbitmqctl list_queues messages_ready
   messages_unacknowledged
   ```

   The response should display our shop queue; details include the name, the number of messages ready to be processed, and one message which has not been acknowledged.

   ```
   Listing queues ...
   shop.queue 9 1
   ...done.
   ```

5. If you press *Ctrl* + *C* while on the command-line console, the consumer script is stopped, and then list the queues again you will notice the message has returned to the queue.

   ```
   Listing queues ...
   shop.queue 10 0
   ...done.
   ```

If you edit the change we made to `consumer.js` script and re-run these steps, the application will work correctly, consuming messages one at a time and sending an acknowledgment to RabbitMQ when each message has been processed.

Publisher Confirms (Intermediate)

This task will look at a RabbitMQ extension to AMQP called **Publisher Confirms** as a way of doing asynchronous transactions.

Getting ready

We mentioned in the previous task, *Persistent messages (Intermediate)*, that there is a short window in which the failure of a RabbitMQ server would result in a message being lost.

The only way to truly guarantee that a message isn't lost is to use AMQP transactions. Since AMQP transactions are synchronous (they block IO) and decrease throughput, we will use Publisher Confirms which is 100 times faster than AMQP transactions. There is more information on the RabbitMQ website (`http://www.rabbitmq.com/confirms.html`) as to why this extension was created.

How to do it...

Let's navigate to our source code examples folder and locate the folder `Publisher-Confirms`. Take a look at the `producer.js` script and examine the changes made to support Publisher Confirms.

1. We pass to the `connect.exchange` function the following options, which tells the connection the channel should be in the confirm mode `confirm:true`:

   ```
   var ex = connect.exchange('shop.exchange', {type: 'direct',
       confirm:true});
   ```

2. When we publish a message, we pass a callback as the last argument. It is here we are able to handle messages that RabbitMQ failed to add to a queue.

   ```
   ex.publish('order.key', newOrder, {deliveryMode:2},
    function(isError){
     if (isError)
     console.log('ERROR, Order has not been acknowledged.');
    });
   ```

Let's demonstrate this concept.

1. Open a command-line console and start RabbitMQ:

   `rabbitmq-server`

2. Now open a command-line console, navigate to our source code examples folder, and locate the folder Publisher-Confirms. Execute the following command:

   `Publisher-Confirms> node producer`

   Messages that RabbitMQ fails to queue will be displayed, although an error will need to be induced in order to see this. Our code will simulate an error on the tenth message, and you should see this message:

   ERROR, Order has not been acknowledged.

Publish Subscribe (Advanced)

The Publish Subscribe pattern allows us to distribute a message to multiple consumer applications from a single producer, allowing us to respond to a single message in multiple ways. This task will demonstrate how we can leverage the Publish Subscribe pattern to improve sHop.

Getting ready

Our sHop application now has a single Work Queue; which we can scale out using multiple consumers. But we can go a step further. The functions `UpdateInventory`, `SendEmail`, and `UpdateReporting` can be executed asynchronously, as they are not dependent on each other. Let's split up these functions and host these on separate consumers.

How to do it...

Let's navigate to our source code examples folder and locate the folder Publish-Subscribe. Here you will find our e-commerce application; it consists of seven files:

- `consumer.js`
- `orderService.js`
- `producer.js`
- `updateInventory.js`
- `updateRecommendations.js`
- `updateReporting.js`
- `sendEmail.js`

Let's take a look at the `orderService.js` script and the `ProcessOrder` function in it.

We have simplified ProcessOrder; the calls to UpdateInventory, SendEmail, and UpdateReporting have been removed as follows:

```
this.ProcessOrder = function() {
  this.PaymentGateway();
  this.UpdateStatus();
  console.log('INFO, Thank you for placing your
  order...');
  return this.Status;
};
```

We will now call each of the preceding functions individually in separate consumer scripts.

Our `producer.js` script has not changed; so let's take a look at the `consumer.js` script, specifically the `q.subscribe` function call:

1. We create a new `OrderService` and call `ProcessOrder`, which now returns the order's `Status`.
2. If the order status equals `OrderComplete`, we create a new `fanout` exchange called `shop.fanout.exchange`, which we use to publish a message.
3. We then call `q.shift`, removing the message from the queue:

```
q.subscribe({ack:true}, function(message) {
  var service = new
  orderService(unescape(message.data));
    var status = service.ProcessOrder();
     if (status === 'OrderComplete') {
       var exf = connect.exchange('shop.fanout.exchange',
{type: 'fanout'});
       exf.setMaxListeners(0);
       exf.publish('', service.Order);
     }
     q.shift();
     console.log('INFO, Remove order from queue.');
    });
```

Our scripts for `updateInventory.js`, `updateReporting.js`, and `sendEmail.js` are basically the same, except they call a different function on the `OrderService` script. Let's take a look at the `SendEmail` script.

1. We create a `fanout` exchange named `shop.fanout.exchange`, which we use to publish a message.
2. We then create a queue named `shop.email.queue`, and wait for the `queueBindOk` event to fire.
3. We call the `q.subscribe` function and create a new `OrderService`.
4. We then call `SendEmail` as follows:

```
connect.on('ready', function() {
    var ex = connect.exchange('shop.fanout.exchange',  {type:
'fanout'});
    var q = connect.queue('shop.email.queue');
    q.on('queueDeclareOk', function(args) {
        q.bind('shop.fanout.exchange', '');
        q.on('queueBindOk', function() {
            q.subscribe(function(message) {
                var service = new
                  orderService(message.data);
                service.SendEmail();
```

```
                    });
                });
            });
        });
```

Let's demonstrate this concept.

1. Open a command-line console and start RabbitMQ:

   `rabbitmq-server`

2. Open a command-line console, navigate to our source code examples folder, and locate the folder `Publish-Subscribe`. Execute each of the following commands in a new command-line console:

   `Publish-Subscribe> node updateInventory`

   `Publish-Subscribe> node sendEmail`

   `Publish-Subscribe> node updateReporting`

   `Publish-Subscribe> node consumer`

   `Publish-Subscribe> node producer`

We now have a producer publishing messages to a consumer, which processes messages/orders. The consumer itself publishes a single message to a `fanout` exchange. All three queues bound to the exchange (`shop.inventory.queue`, `shop.reporting.queue`, and `shop.email.queue`) receive the message and react to it in their own way.

How it works...

The following diagram demonstrates the concept. The producer publishes a message to the Fanout Exchange with an empty routing key. The Fanout Exchange simply forwards the message to all queues bound to the exchange. In this example, all consumers receive a copy of the message. A Fanout Exchange has the simplest routing algorithm of the AMQP exchanges, giving it the best performance:

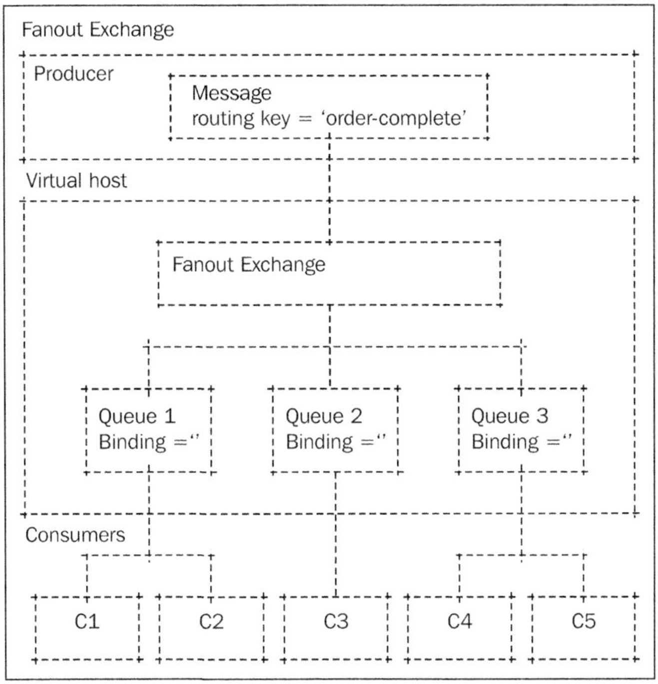

There's more...

Our product owners at sHop have decided to add a recommendation service to sHop. When an order is placed, our `order` processor will need to update the recommendation's database. Let's add this new function to `OrderService`:

```
this.UpdateRecommendations = function() {
  console.log('INFO, Updated recommendations');
};
```

Now we create a new consumer, which is bound to `shop.fanout.exchange` and calls `UpdateRecommendations`:

```
connect.on('ready', function() {
    var ex = connect.exchange('shop.fanout.exchange',  {type:
'fanout'});
    var q = connect.queue('shop.recommendations.queue');
    q.on('queueDeclareOk', function(args) {
        q.bind('shop.fanout.exchange', '');
        q.on('queueBindOk', function() {
            q.subscribe(function(message) {
                var service = new
                  orderService(message.data);
```

```
                    service.UpdateRecommendations();
                });
            });
        });
    });
```

And there we have it; we have extended our sHop application by simply adding a new consumer. Follow the preceding steps to run this example. Open another command-line console to run `updateRecommendations`.

```
Publish-Subscribe> node updateRecommendations
```

Complex routing (Advanced)

In this task, we will decouple our application further by splitting up sHop's logging. We will use a topic exchange to implement a variation of the Publish Subscribe pattern, routing different types of messages to multiple queues.

Getting ready

Let's decouple the various levels of logging our sHop application uses. We have three loggers, each represents a function within our sHop organization. Each function is interested in different types of message/logs:

Logger	Levels	Binding	Description
Fulfillment	ERROR	`Order.log.ERROR`	Errors from orders
Developer	ERROR	`*.log.ERROR`	Errors from everywhere
Operations	ERROR, WARN, INFO	`*.log.*`	Everything from Everywhere

How to do it...

Let's navigate to our source code examples and locate the folder `Complex-Routing`. You will find our e-commerce application; consisting of 11 files:

- `consumer.js`
- `developerLog.js`
- `fulfilmentLog.js`
- `loggingService.js`
- `operationsLog.js`
- `orderService.js`

- `producer.js`
- `updateInventory.js`
- `updateRecommendations.js`
- `updateReporting.js`
- `sendEmail.js`

Let's take a look at the `loggingService.js` module; it's basically a producer.

1. We export a single function called `Log`, which accepts three parameters: `location`, `level`, and `message`.
2. Now we import the `amqp` module and call `createConnection` on that module, returning a connection to the RabbitMQ server.
3. We wait on a connection `ready` event.
4. When the ready event fires we create an exchange. We name the exchange `logging.exchange` and specify the exchange type `topic`.

   ```
   var ex = connect.exchange('logging.exchange', {type: 'topic'});
   ```

5. We define a queue named `logging.queue`, and we bind it to `logging.exchange` as follows:

   ```
   var q = connect.queue('logging.queue');
   q.bind('logging.exchange');
   ```

6. We publish `message` with a routing key, which is a concatenation of the `location` and `level` parameters.

   ```
   module.exports = function Logging() {
     this.Log = function (location, level, message) {
       var connect = require('amqp').createConnection();
         connect.on('ready', function() {
         var ex = connect.exchange('logging.exchange', {type:
   'topic'});
         var q = connect.queue('logging.queue');
         q.on('queueDeclareOk', function(args) {
           q.bind('logging.exchange');
           q.on('queueBindOk', function() {
             ex.publish(location + '.log.' + level, message);
             });
           });
         });
       };
     };
   ```

Let's take a look at the `fulfilmentLog.js` script; it's basically a consumer. Each of our three loggers follow this pattern, so we will not repeat all three:

1. We define an exchange of the type `topic`.

   ```
   var ex = connect.exchange('logging.exchange', {type: 'topic'});
   ```

2. Each logger has its own queue; we name this queue `order.logging.queue`.

   ```
   var q = connect.queue('fulfilment.logging.queue');
   ```

3. Importantly, when we bind the exchange to the queue, we specify the binding key `Order.log.ERROR`.

   ```
   q.bind('logging.exchange', 'Order.log.ERROR');
   ```

4. For the purpose of this example, the logger simply publishes to console:

   ```
     connect.on('ready', function() {
       var ex = connect.exchange('logging.exchange', {type:
   'topic'});
       var q = connect.queue('fulfilment.logging.queue');
       q.on('queueDeclareOk', function(args) {
           q.bind('logging.exchange', 'Order.log.ERROR');
           q.on('queueBindOk', function() {
               q.subscribe(function(message) {
                   console.log(message.data.toString());
               });
           });
         });
     });
   ```

Now, let's complete the picture and take a look at the `orderService.js` script.

1. First, we import and create `loggingService`.
2. Now instead of using `console.log`, we pass our messages to the `logger.log` function as follows:

   ```
   var loggingService = require('./loggingService');
   var logger = new loggingService();

   module.exports = function OrderService(order) {
       this.Order = order;
       this.Checkout = function() {
       logger.Log("Checkout", "INFO", "Placed order " + this.Order.
   OrderId);
       };
       this.ProcessOrder = function() {
         this.PaymentGateway();
         this.UpdateStatus();
   ```

```
      logger.Log("ProcessOrder", "INFO", "Thank you for placing
your order");
      return this.Status;
    };
    this.PaymentGateway = function() {
      logger.Log("PaymentGateway", "INFO", "Made payment");
      this.Status = "OrderComplete";
    };
    this.UpdateStatus = function() {
      logger.Log("UpdateStatus", "INFO", "Updated status");
    };
    this.UpdateInventory = function() {
      logger.Log("UpdateInventory", "INFO", "Update inventory");
    };
    this.SendEmail = function() {
      logger.Log("SendEmail", "INFO", "Sent email");
    };
    this.UpdateReporting = function() {
      logger.Log("UpdateReporting", "INFO", "Updated reporting");
    };
    this.UpdateRecommendations = function() {
      logger.Log("UpdateRecommendations", "INFO", "Updated
recommendations");
    };
  };
```

3. Open a command-line console and start RabbitMQ:

   rabbitmq-server

4. Open a command-line console, navigate to our source code examples folder, and locate the folder Complex-Routing. Execute each of the following commands in a new command-line console:

   Complex-Routing> node updateInventory

   Complex-Routing> node sendEmail

   Complex-Routing> node updateReporting

   Complex-Routing> node updateRecommendations

   Complex-Routing> node developerLog

   Complex-Routing> node operationsLog

   Complex-Routing> node fulfilmentLog

   Complex-Routing> node consumer

   Complex-Routing> node producer

Now, when we run this example all the output is directed to the three loggers. Each logger receives only the messages it's interested in. `operationsLog` receives all the messages.

How it works...

The Topic Exchange algorithm performs a wildcard match between the routing key and the routing pattern specified in the binding. The routing key must be a list of words, delimited by dots. Our example uses `Order.ERROR`, `*.ERROR`, and so on. The following diagram explains this:

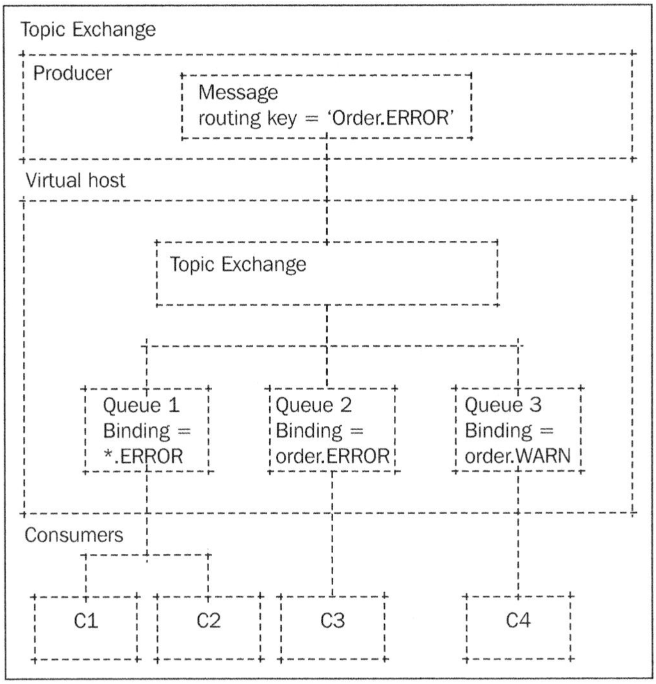

A message sent with a particular routing key will be delivered to all the queues that are bound with a matching binding key. However, a Topic Exchange has two special cases for binding keys as follows:

- * (star) matches one word
- # (hash) matches zero or more words

Go forth and multiply

The topics we have covered in this book are centered around application development. This task will provide you with a series of further topics to research and consider when building and deploying applications using RabbitMQ.

Clustering and Mirrored Queues

We looked at various options for reliable message delivery, but what if the RabbitMQ server fails? What if it does not restart? RabbitMQ provides options for ensuring availability when a failure occurs; it has built-in support for **Clustering** (`www.rabbitmq.com/clustering.html`).

Clustering only solves a part of the problem. Nodes in a cluster do not store multiple copies of messages. There is only one queue and one copy of the messages in a cluster of nodes. What happens if the node with the queue fails? RabbitMQ supports **Mirrored Queues** (`www.rabbitmq.com/ha.html`).

Mirrored Queues allow us to replicate their contents across all nodes in a cluster; all the communication goes through the master node, which replicates to slaves. If the master fails, a new master node is selected (the oldest node in the cluster) and the service resumes with no unavailability of service.

Error handling and recovery

Messaging applications have to contend with different types of failure, including; RabbitMQ outage, network connection interruption, and AMQP entity-level exceptions. Handling failure and attempting to recover is not an easy thing to do.

Node.js applications have rightly embraced crash-only design (crash/log/restart). This is seen as a pragmatic approach; it avoids having to recover from an unknown state and reduces memory leaks.

By adding the following connection handlers, we can implement a crash-only design pattern. The following closes a process when a connection is closed:

```
connection.on("close", function() {
  console.log("Closing connection")
  process.exit(1);
});
```

This handler closes a process when a connection errors:

```
connection.on("error", function(err) {
  console.log("Error: ", err)
  process.exit(1);
});
```

A Node.js application takes milliseconds to start; we can use a process monitoring system like one of the following to restart a process:

- Monit (`www.mmonit.com/monit`)
- Upstart (`upstart.ubuntu.com`)
- npm forever (`www.npmjs.org/package/forever`)
- npm up (`www.npmjs.org/package/up`)

Starting up process(s) on other platforms such as Java/.NET is a little more expensive, so this technique is probably not an option. We would on these platforms be looking to failover by catching errors or detecting closed connections and attempting to reconnect.

AMQP connections

AMQP connections, as previously mentioned, are an expensive resource to create. AMQP has a concept of channels, which provide a way to multiplex a heavyweight TCP/IP connection into several lightweight connections. What we would ideally like to do is share a connection across the application, although this is not always possible. For example. in a cloud-based worker scenario. you need to create and rip down a connection on request.

Connections are also a finite resource; the number of concurrent connections a RabbitMQ server will allow is less than 1,000. In order to increase this, we need to tune `ulimit`, which will increase the number of **file descriptors**; the max is 32 K. Also bare in mind that each queue you create will use one file descriptor.

Heartbeats

Heartbeats are an important AMQP concept, which help us to control the life span of active connections. An AMQP client can be configured to send heartbeat frames at a predefined interval when the connection is idle. This heartbeat frame is simply a way for a client to tell the server that the connection is still active.

If the server does not receive a heartbeat within that interval, it will close the connection. If the server does receive a heartbeat in that timeframe, it will send back a heartbeat frame to the client. The following configuration sets the heartbeat to 600 seconds (10 minutes), which is also the AMQP default value for long running connections:

```
var options = {
  host: 'localhost' , port: 5672 , login: 'guest' , password: 'guest'
, vhost: '/'
};

options.heartbeat = 600;
var connect = require('amqp').createConnection(options);
```

Heartbeats can also be used to safely end a short-lived connection. The following configuration sets the heartbeat to 120 seconds (2 minutes), and ends the connection when the client receives a heartbeat response.

```
var options = {
  host: 'localhost' , port: 5672 , login: 'guest' , password: 'guest'
, vhost: '/'
};

options.heartbeat = 120;
var connect = require('amqp').createConnection(options);

connection.on("heartbeat", function() {
  this.end();
});
```

In order to disable heartbeats, simply set the heartbeat value to `0`.

AMQP Reconnects

Reconnects allow us to attempt a reconnection after losing a network connection to RabbitMQ. In this scenario the connection is still alive in RabbitMQ. Reconnects are easily configured with the following additions to the connection's `options` object.

```
options.reconnect = true;
options.reconnectBackoffTime = 500;
options.reconnectBackoffStrategy = "exponential";
```

Configuration

Our examples have relied on RabbitMQ's default configuration, which will probably be sufficient for running your RabbitMQ server. There are options for configuring RabbitMQ described at `www.rabbitmq.com/configure.html`.

AMQP 1.0

You may be asking yourself why RabbitMQ does not implement the AMQP 1.0 specification. AMQP 1.0 is a completely different protocol to AMQP 0-9-1.
Read more here: `www.rabbitmq.com/specification.html`

Hosting

Managing your own RabbitMQ instance can be time consuming. If you would like to avoid this, I can highly recommend `www.cloudamqp.com`, which support a free tier (two-connection) RabbitMQ service, and lots of paid options for larger rabbits.

Architecture and performance

The architecture and your connection/exchange/queue configuration choices will impact the overall performance of your application. In conclusion please consider the following points; now go forth and multiply:

- RabbitMQ connections are a finite resource; the number of active connections should be controlled.
- The file descriptor limit will determine how many concurrent connections your rabbit can handle.
- Each queue you create consumes one file descriptor.
- The exchange type due to their algorithm implementations impact performance.
- A Topic Exchange, due to its complex routing algorithm, does not perform as well as say a Fanout or Direct Exchange. Topic Exchanges are useful when we have an infinite number of routing keys.
- In terms of memory cost, exchanges and bindings are cheap.
- RabbitMQ will perform better if a message reaches an empty queue; you should not leave messages in a queue for a long time.
- When we have a small number of consumers, adding more will increase performance.
- Small messages will be consumed faster than larger messages.
- When queues are small, they will reside entirely within the memory.
- When queues get larger, they will get paged to disc regardless of your options to persist.
- Small prefetch counts can hurt performance, as we are waiting for acknowledgements to arrive before sending out more messages.
- When we have a larger prefetch count, increasing the number of consumers does not have the same impact.
- When using Topic Exchange; binding using the `*` wildcard is much faster than the # wildcard.
- RabbitMQ Publisher Confirms are more than 100 times faster than AMQP transactions.

Thank you for buying
Instant RabbitMQ Messaging Application Development How-to

About Packt Publishing

Packt, pronounced 'packed', published its first book "*Mastering phpMyAdmin for Effective MySQL Management*" in April 2004 and subsequently continued to specialize in publishing highly focused books on specific technologies and solutions.

Our books and publications share the experiences of your fellow IT professionals in adapting and customizing today's systems, applications, and frameworks. Our solution based books give you the knowledge and power to customize the software and technologies you're using to get the job done. Packt books are more specific and less general than the IT books you have seen in the past. Our unique business model allows us to bring you more focused information, giving you more of what you need to know, and less of what you don't.

Packt is a modern, yet unique publishing company, which focuses on producing quality, cutting-edge books for communities of developers, administrators, and newbies alike. For more information, please visit our website: `www.packtpub.com`.

Writing for Packt

We welcome all inquiries from people who are interested in authoring. Book proposals should be sent to `author@packtpub.com`. If your book idea is still at an early stage and you would like to discuss it first before writing a formal book proposal, contact us; one of our commissioning editors will get in touch with you.

We're not just looking for published authors; if you have strong technical skills but no writing experience, our experienced editors can help you develop a writing career, or simply get some additional reward for your expertise.

[PACKT] PUBLISHING

ZeroMQ

ISBN: 978-1-78216-104-2 Paperback: 108 pages

Use ZeroMQ and learn how to apply different message patterns

1. Learn fundamental message/queue design patterns
2. Work with multi-threaded programs
3. Work with multiple sockets

Django JavaScript Integration: AJAX and jQuery

ISBN: 978-1-84951-034-9 Paperback: 324 pages

Develop AJAX applications using Django and jQuery

1. Learn how Django + jQuery = AJAX
2. Integrate your AJAX application with Django on the server side and jQuery on the client side
3. Learn how to handle AJAX requests with jQuery
4. Compare the pros and cons of client-side search with JavaScript and initializing a search on the server side via AJAX
5. Handle login and authentication via Django-based AJAX

Please check **www.PacktPub.com** for information on our titles

[PACKT]
PUBLISHING

Drush User's Guide

ISBN: 978-1-84951-798-0 Paperback: 140 pages

A practical guide to Drush, Drupal's command line interface, helping you work with your Drupal sites more effectively

1. Stop clicking around administration pages and start issuing commands straight to your Drupal sites
2. Write your own commands, hook in to alter existing ones and extend the toolkit with a long list of contributed modules
3. A practical guide full of examples and step-by-step instructions to start using Drush right from Chapter 1

Django 1.2 e-commerce

ISBN: 978-1-84719-700-9 Paperback: 244 pages

Build powerful e-commerce applications using Django, a leading Python web framework

1. Build all the components for an e-commerce store, from product catalog to shopping cart to checkout processor
2. Build a high quality e-commerce site quickly and start making money
3. All the examples in the book will run smoothly for all the versions of Django 1.x
4. Follow a tutorial format to build many components from scratch while leveraging the open-source community to enhance functionality

Please check **www.PacktPub.com** for information on our titles

Printed in Dunstable, United Kingdom

91218877R00031